Adult
MAD LIBS®

The world's greatest _gangster_ game

Scarface Mad Libs

by Brian D. Clark

PSS!
PRICE STERN SLOAN
An Imprint of Penguin Random House

PRICE STERN SLOAN
An Imprint of Penguin Random House LLC

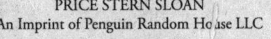

Mad Libs format copyright © 2015 by Price Stern Sloan, an imprint of Penguin Random House LLC. All rights reserved.

Concept created by Roger Price & Leonard Stern.

© 2015 Universal Studios Licensing LLC. Scarface copyright of Universal Studios. All rights reserved.

Published by Price Stern Sloan,
an imprint of Penguin Random House LLC,
345 Hudson Street, New York, New York 10014,
Printed in the USA.

ISBN 978-0-8431-8239-2

1 3 5 7 9 10 8 6 4 2

Adult MAD LIBS® INSTRUCTIONS

The world's greatest _gangster_ game

MAD LIBS® is a game for people who don't like games!
It can be played by one, two, three, four, or forty.

• RIDICULOUSLY SIMPLE DIRECTIONS

In this book, you'll find stories containing blank spaces where words are left out. One player, the READER, selects one of the stories. The READER shouldn't tell anyone what the story is about. Instead, the READER should ask the other players, the WRITERS, to give words to fill in the blank spaces in the story.

• TO PLAY

The READER asks each WRITER in turn to call out words—adjectives or nouns or whatever the spaces call for—and uses them to fill in the blank spaces in the story. The result is your very own MAD LIBS! Then, when the READER reads the completed MAD LIBS to the other players, they will discover they have written a story that is fantastic, screamingly funny, shocking, silly, crazy, or just plain dumb—depending on the words each WRITER called out.

• EXAMPLE (*Before* and *After*)

" _____ !" he said _____
      EXCLAMATION   ADVERB

as he jumped into his convertible _____ and
                                                NOUN

drove off with his _____ wife.
                              ADJECTIVE

" _Ouch_ !" he said _stupidly_
      EXCLAMATION   ADVERB

as he jumped into his convertible _cat_ and
                                                NOUN

drove off with his _brave_ wife.
                              ADJECTIVE

In case you have forgotten what adjectives, adverbs, nouns, and verbs are, here is a quick review:

An **ADJECTIVE** describes something or somebody. *Lumpy, soft, ugly, messy,* and *short* are adjectives.

An **ADVERB** tells how something is done. It modifies a verb and usually ends in "ly." *Modestly, stupidly, greedily,* and *carefully* are adverbs.

A **NOUN** is the name of a person, place, or thing. *Sidewalk, umbrella, bridle, bathtub,* and *nose* are nouns.

A **VERB** is an action word. *Run, pitch, jump,* and *swim* are verbs. Put the verbs in past tense if the directions say **PAST TENSE.** *Ran, pitched, jumped,* and *swam* are verbs in the past tense.

When we ask for **A PLACE,** we mean any sort of place: a country or city (*Spain, Cleveland*) or a room (*bathroom, kitchen*).

An **EXCLAMATION** or **SILLY WORD** is any sort of funny sound, gasp, grunt, or outcry, like *Wow!, Ouch!, Whomp!, Ick!,* and *Gadzooks!*

When we ask for specific words, like a **NUMBER,** a **COLOR,** an **ANIMAL,** or a **PART OF THE BODY,** we mean a word that is one of those things, like *seven, blue, horse,* or *head.*

When we ask for a **PLURAL,** it means more than one. For example, *cat* pluralized is *cats.*

Adult MAD LIBS® GET SCARFACED

The world's greatest _gangster_ game

MAD LIBS® is fun to play with friends, but you can also play it by yourself! To begin with, DO NOT look at the story on the page below. Fill in the blanks on this page with the words called for. Then, using the words you have selected, fill in the blank spaces in the story. Now you've created your own hilarious MAD LIBS® game!

ADJECTIVE _____

NOUN _____

ADJECTIVE _____

ADJECTIVE _____

OCCUPATION _____

A PLACE _____

NUMBER _____

NOUN _____

PART OF THE BODY _____

ADVERB _____

VERB ENDING IN "ING" _____

ADJECTIVE _____

VERB ENDING IN "ING" _____

PLURAL NOUN _____

NOUN _____

SILLY WORD _____

VERB _____

NOUN _____

Can't remember all the ＿＿＿＿＿＿ twists and turns found in the

ADJECTIVE

plot of ＿＿＿＿＿＿-*face*? Well, here's your chance to revisit the

NOUN

story of this ＿＿＿＿＿＿ Hollywood film. *Scarface* follows the

ADJECTIVE

＿＿＿＿＿＿ life of a gun-wielding ＿＿＿＿＿＿ named Tony

ADJECTIVE · OCCUPATION

(the) ＿＿＿＿＿＿, a Cuban immigrant who will stop at nothing

A PLACE

to become Miami's number ＿＿＿＿ ＿＿＿＿＿＿ dealer. When

NUMBER · NOUN

Tony first sets ＿＿＿＿＿＿ in America, he ＿＿＿＿＿＿ realizes

PART OF THE BODY · ADVERB

that ＿＿＿＿＿＿ dishes isn't for him. So, he and his ＿＿＿＿＿＿

VERB ENDING IN "ING" · ADJECTIVE

friend Manny start ＿＿＿＿＿＿ and selling illegal ＿＿＿＿＿＿.

VERB ENDING IN "ING" · PLURAL NOUN

Before long, Tony is in love with his boss's ＿＿＿＿＿＿ and

NOUN

plotting his own drug empire, with the help of a Bolivian drug lord

named Alejandro ＿＿＿＿＿＿. Sadly, things don't go according to

SILLY WORD

plan for Tony after he deliberately doesn't ＿＿＿＿＿＿ a journalist

VERB

and ends up shot to death inside his opulent ＿＿＿＿＿＿.

NOUN

Adult
MAD LIBS®
FREEDOM TOWN RULES OF CONDUCT

The world's greatest _gangster_ game

MAD LIBS® is fun to play with friends, but you can also play it by yourself! To begin with, DO NOT look at the story on the page below. Fill in the blanks on this page with the words called for. Then, using the words you have selected, fill in the blank spaces in the story. Now you've created your own hilarious MAD LIBS® game!

ADJECTIVE _____

NUMBER _____

A PLACE _____

ADJECTIVE _____

PLURAL NOUN _____

VERB _____

PART OF THE BODY _____

ANIMAL (PLURAL) _____

ADJECTIVE _____

NOUN _____

VERB ENDING IN "ING" _____

NOUN _____

ADJECTIVE _____

VERB _____

NOUN _____

COLOR _____

NOUN _____

Adult MAD LIBS®

FREEDOM TOWN RULES OF CONDUCT

The world's greatest _gangster_ game

Welcome to _____ Town! To keep from getting killed while
                    ADJECTIVE

locked up in this refugee camp under Interstate _____ in (the)
                                                    NUMBER

_____, you'll need to remember a few _____ rules . . .
   A PLACE   ADJECTIVE

1. Keep your friends close and your _____ closer!
                                      PLURAL NOUN

2. Always _____ with one _____ open.
             VERB   PART OF THE BODY

3. When a riot breaks out, avoid barking police _____ and
                                                   ANIMAL (PLURAL)

   _____-pressure _____ hoses at all costs.
      ADJECTIVE   NOUN

4. Your mattress can be used for more than just _____ on!
                                                  VERB ENDING IN "ING"

   Try using it to scale a barbed _____ fence or beat it with a
                                     NOUN

   stick to terrorize _____ government officials.
                         ADJECTIVE

5. And always remember to _____ a communist with a sharp
                             VERB

   _____ if you want to get your _____ card! That's
      NOUN   COLOR

   your _____ to freedom!
           NOUN

Adult MAD LIBS®

THE REVIEWS ARE IN

The world's greatest _gangster_ game

MAD LIBS® is fun to play with friends, but you can also play it by yourself! To begin with, DO NOT look at the story on the page below. Fill in the blanks on this page with the words called for. Then, using the words you have selected, fill in the blank spaces in the story. Now you've created your own hilarious MAD LIBS® game!

NUMBER _____

PART OF THE BODY _____

ADJECTIVE _____

EXCLAMATION _____

VEHICLE _____

NOUN _____

A PLACE _____

CELEBRITY (MALE) _____

NOUN _____

CELEBRITY (FEMALE) _____

ADVERB _____

ANIMAL _____

PART OF THE BODY _____

TYPE OF LIQUID _____

SILLY WORD _____

NOUN _____

VERB _____

Adult
MAD LIBS®
THE REVIEWS ARE IN

The world's greatest ___gangster___ game

Here's a/an _____-star review of *Scar-_____*,
⠀⠀⠀⠀⠀⠀⠀⠀⠀ NUMBER ⠀⠀⠀⠀⠀⠀⠀⠀⠀⠀⠀⠀⠀⠀⠀⠀⠀ PART OF THE BODY

straight from the archives of the _____ *York Times* entertainment
⠀⠀⠀⠀⠀⠀⠀⠀⠀⠀⠀⠀⠀⠀⠀⠀⠀⠀⠀⠀⠀⠀⠀⠀⠀⠀⠀⠀ ADJECTIVE

section . . .

December 9, 1983

_____! If you do anything this weekend, make sure you get
⠀⠀ EXCLAMATION

in your _____, buy a ticket for a front-_____
⠀⠀⠀⠀⠀⠀⠀ VEHICLE ⠀⠀⠀⠀⠀⠀⠀⠀⠀⠀⠀⠀⠀⠀⠀⠀⠀⠀⠀⠀⠀⠀ NOUN

seat at your local _____, and experience *Scarface*.
⠀⠀⠀⠀⠀⠀⠀⠀⠀⠀⠀⠀⠀⠀⠀ A PLACE

_____ is brilliant as the film's leading _____
⠀ CELEBRITY (MALE) ⠀⠀⠀⠀⠀⠀⠀⠀⠀⠀⠀⠀⠀⠀⠀⠀⠀⠀⠀⠀⠀⠀⠀⠀⠀ NOUN

and _____ as Elvira is _____ breathtaking to
⠀⠀⠀⠀ CELEBRITY (FEMALE) ⠀⠀⠀⠀⠀⠀⠀⠀⠀⠀⠀⠀⠀ ADVERB

watch as she slinks around like a/an _____ in heat! But, be
⠀⠀⠀⠀⠀⠀⠀⠀⠀⠀⠀⠀⠀⠀⠀⠀⠀⠀⠀⠀⠀⠀⠀⠀⠀⠀⠀⠀ ANIMAL

warned, this movie is not for the faint of _____. The
⠀⠀⠀⠀⠀⠀⠀⠀⠀⠀⠀⠀⠀⠀⠀⠀⠀⠀⠀⠀⠀⠀⠀⠀⠀⠀⠀ PART OF THE BODY

_____-soaked action sequences are brutal, and expletives
⠀ TYPE OF LIQUID

like _____ are bandied about almost as often as rounds
⠀⠀⠀ SILLY WORD

of _____ are shot out of a machine gun! It's *the* must-
⠀⠀⠀ NOUN

_____ movie of the year!
⠀ VERB

Adult
MAD LIBS
DRUG DEAL GONE BAD

The world's greatest _gangster_ game

MAD LIBS® is fun to play with friends, but you can also play it by yourself! To begin with, DO NOT look at the story on the page below. Fill in the blanks on this page with the words called for. Then, using the words you have selected, fill in the blank spaces in the story. Now you've created your own hilarious MAD LIBS® game!

ADJECTIVE _____

FIRST NAME (MALE) _____

ADJECTIVE _____

NOUN _____

ADJECTIVE _____

OCCUPATION (PLURAL) _____

NOUN _____

SILLY WORD (PLURAL) _____

NOUN _____

FIRST NAME (MALE) _____

VERB (PAST TENSE) _____

ADVERB _____

SILLY WORD _____

SAME SILLY WORD _____

NOUN _____

Drug deals are difficult, even under the most _____
_____ADJECTIVE_____

circumstances. _____ Montana learned this lesson the
_____FIRST NAME (MALE)_____

_____ way in a Miami Beach _____ while on his
__ADJECTIVE__   __NOUN__

first big job. The deal turned _____ when he and his fellow
_____ADJECTIVE_____

_____ found themselves held at _____-point
__OCCUPATION (PLURAL)__   __NOUN__

by a rival dealer and his group of _____, and only got
_____SILLY WORD (PLURAL)_____

worse when Tony discovered that the guy trying to buy the cocaine

had a/an _____ in his briefcase. Moments later, Tony's friend
_____NOUN_____

_____ got _____ to pieces in the bathroom and
__FIRST NAME (MALE)__   __VERB (PAST TENSE)__

it looked like Tony would be next! _____, Tony's friends
_____ADVERB_____

Manny and _____ _____ came to the
_____SILLY WORD_____   __SAME SILLY WORD__

rescue, and Tony made it out alive with the cash and a few kilos of

_____.
__NOUN__

DIRECTOR'S TO-DO LIST

The world's greatest _gangster_ game

MAD LIBS® is fun to play with friends, but you can also play it by yourself! To begin with, DO NOT look at the story on the page below. Fill in the blanks on this page with the words called for. Then, using the words you have selected, fill in the blank spaces in the story. Now you've created your own hilarious MAD LIBS® game!

VERB _____

PERSON IN ROOM (FEMALE) _____

CELEBRITY (FEMALE) _____

ADJECTIVE _____

ADJECTIVE _____

OCCUPATION _____

A PLACE _____

ADJECTIVE _____

NOUN _____

A PLACE _____

LETTER OF THE ALPHABET _____

ADJECTIVE _____

NOUN _____

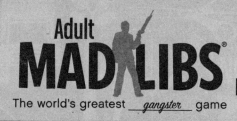

Adult MAD LIBS®

DIRECTOR'S TO-DO LIST

The world's greatest __gangster__ game

Here's a page ripped straight from the production notebook of the

Scarface director:

To-_____ List:
      VERB

1. For the part of Elvira, see if _____ is available. If
                                    PERSON IN ROOM (FEMALE)

   not, we could always settle for _____, though
                                    CELEBRITY (FEMALE)

   she's kind of _____ for the role, or just hire a very
                   ADJECTIVE

   _____ but unknown actress.
   ADJECTIVE

2. Try to convince the _____ of Miami to allow me
                        OCCUPATION

   to shoot on location. If he thinks the movie portrays (the)

   _____ in a/an _____ light, move production
   A PLACE   ADJECTIVE

   back to Holly-_____.
                   NOUN

3. Call the Motion Picture Association of (the) _____ and
                                               A PLACE

   find out why they keep giving the film a/an _____
                                               LETTER OF THE ALPHABET

   rating. Then, edit out the really _____ violence, so
                                      ADJECTIVE

   the film can be released on _____.
                                NOUN

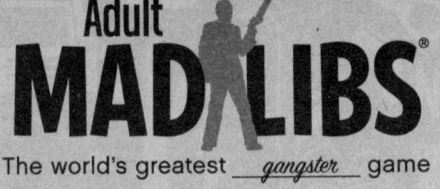

Adult MAD LIBS®

TONY'S ANGER-MANAGEMENT CLASS

The world's greatest _gangster_ game

MAD LIBS® is fun to play with friends, but you can also play it by yourself! To begin with, DO NOT look at the story on the page below. Fill in the blanks on this page with the words called for. Then, using the words you have selected, fill in the blank spaces in the story. Now you've created your own hilarious MAD LIBS® game!

VERB ENDING IN "ING" _____

ADJECTIVE _____

PLURAL NOUN _____

VERB ENDING IN "ING" _____

PART OF THE BODY _____

NUMBER _____

ADJECTIVE _____

ADJECTIVE _____

VERB (PAST TENSE) _____

NOUN _____

ADJECTIVE _____

TYPE OF LIQUID _____

VERB _____

NOUN _____

Adult MAD LIBS®

TONY'S ANGER-MANAGEMENT CLASS

The world's greatest _gangster_ game

To be a successful gangster, you've got to know how to control your

anger—otherwise, it will end up _____ you! Here are
_{VERB ENDING IN "ING"}

Tony's suggestions on how to deal with all that _____ rage
_{ADJECTIVE}

you've built up inside . . .

Never resort to violence to solve your _____ . Instead, try to
_{PLURAL NOUN}

talk out your feelings with rival thugs before _____ them
_{VERB ENDING IN "ING"}

in the _____ . Take a/an _____-minute "time-
_{PART OF THE BODY}   _{NUMBER}

out" to consider your options before making _____ decisions,
_{ADJECTIVE}

like when deciding whether to kill your _____ friend in a fit of
_{ADJECTIVE}

jealous rage because he _____ your sister. If you find yourself
_{VERB (PAST TENSE)}

losing your _____, remember to take _____ cleansing
_{NOUN}   _{ADJECTIVE}

breaths before attacking your girlfriend in a restaurant. Do not use

drugs or _____ to deal with your problems. They impair your
_{TYPE OF LIQUID}

ability to _____ clearly . . . and will likely make it harder to
_{VERB}

aim that _____ launcher.
_{NOUN}

Adult MAD LIBS

WRITING IS REWRITING

The world's greatest _gangster_ game

MAD LIBS® is fun to play with friends, but you can also play it by yourself! To begin with, DO NOT look at the story on the page below. Fill in the blanks on this page with the words called for. Then, using the words you have selected, fill in the blank spaces in the story. Now you've created your own hilarious MAD LIBS® game!

ADJECTIVE _____

ADJECTIVE _____

VERB ENDING IN "S" _____

ADVERB _____

NOUN _____

VERB ENDING IN "ING" _____

PART OF THE BODY _____

PLURAL NOUN _____

VERB ENDING IN "ING" _____

PART OF THE BODY (PLURAL) _____

ADJECTIVE _____

ADJECTIVE _____

VERB _____

NOUN _____

VERB _____

NOUN _____

Adult MAD LIBS®

WRITING IS REWRITING

The world's greatest ___gangster___ game

We've just secured this page from the masterful *Scarface* script. Take a

look at one of Tony's _____ monologues . . .
ADJECTIVE

INT. _____ RESTAURANT—NIGHT
ADJECTIVE

Tony _____ across the room, _____ intoxicated.
VERB ENDING IN "S" _ADVERB_

Patrons stare at him as he crosses to the _____.
NOUN

TONY: What you lookin' at? You all a bunch of _____
VERB ENDING IN "ING"

_____-holes. You know why? You don't have the guts
PART OF THE BODY

to be what you want to be. You need _____ like me. You
PLURAL NOUN

need people like me so you can point your _____
VERB ENDING IN "ING"

_____ and say, "That's the _____ guy." So, what does
PART OF THE BODY (PLURAL) _ADJECTIVE_

that make you? Good? You're not _____. You just know how to
ADJECTIVE

hide . . . and _____. Me, I don't have that _____. Me,
VERB _NOUN_

I always tell the truth. Even when I _____! So say good night
VERB

to the bad _____!
NOUN

MAD LIBS® is fun to play with friends, but you can also play it by yourself! To begin with, DO NOT look at the story on the page below. Fill in the blanks on this page with the words called for. Then, using the words you have selected, fill in the blank spaces in the story. Now you've created your own hilarious MAD LIBS® game!

ADJECTIVE _____

NUMBER _____

NOUN _____

VERB ENDING IN "ING" _____

PLURAL NOUN _____

NOUN _____

PLURAL NOUN _____

COLOR _____

VERB ENDING IN "ING" _____

ADJECTIVE _____

ADJECTIVE _____

FIRST NAME (FEMALE) _____

NOUN _____

Adult MAD LIBS®   FAMILY REUNION

The world's greatest _gangster_ game

Family reunions can be _____, especially if you've been locked
                            ADJECTIVE

away for _____ years in a Cuban _____—and if your
            NUMBER   NOUN

mother knows about your habit of _____ people and
                                  VERB ENDING IN "ING"

selling _____. At least, that's what Tony discovered when
            PLURAL NOUN

he visited his mother's _____ in Miami in the hopes of
                        NOUN

buying back his family's love with $1,000 in _____ and a/an
                                        PLURAL NOUN

_____ locket. But, despite Tony's attempts to reconcile, his
    COLOR

mother ended up _____ her son out of her house forever!
                    VERB ENDING IN "ING"

On the _____ side, the meeting did reunite Tony with his
          ADJECTIVE

_____ sister, _____, whom he hadn't seen since
    ADJECTIVE   FIRST NAME (FEMALE)

she was a small _____.
                NOUN

MAD LIBS® is fun to play with friends, but you can also play it by yourself! To begin with, DO NOT look at the story on the page below. Fill in the blanks on this page with the words called for. Then, using the words you have selected, fill in the blank spaces in the story. Now you've created your own hilarious MAD LIBS® game!

NOUN _____

COLOR _____

ADJECTIVE _____

NOUN _____

VERB ENDING IN "ING" _____

ARTICLE OF CLOTHING (PLURAL) _____

NOUN _____

NUMBER _____

ADJECTIVE _____

ADJECTIVE _____

NOUN _____

SILLY WORD _____

PART OF THE BODY _____

NOUN _____

NOUN _____

Adult

MAD LIBS®

The world's greatest _gangster_ game

ELVIRA HANCOCK'S PERSONALS AD

Elvira will do anything to find her next hit of _____, even
NOUN

post this personals ad . . .

Single female _____ digger/addict seeks _____
COLOR   ADJECTIVE

drug lord for long-term _____. You must like fine
NOUN

_____ at top restaurants, buying me slutty but expensive
VERB ENDING IN "ING"

evening _____, and bitter conversations by
ARTICLE OF CLOTHING (PLURAL)

_____-light. Must also drive a Porsche _____ or
NOUN   NUMBER

better. Gangsters with _____ heritage and a/an _____
ADJECTIVE   ADJECTIVE

sense of humor a plus. My hobbies include lounging by the built-

in _____ at your mansion, getting _____ off my
NOUN   SILLY WORD

_____, not earning my own _____, and cheating
PART OF THE BODY   NOUN

on my _____ as soon as someone better comes along.
NOUN

Adult MAD LIBS®

TRAVEL TO BOLIVIA TODAY!

The world's greatest _gangster_ game

MAD LIBS® is fun to play with friends, but you can also play it by yourself! To begin with, DO NOT look at the story on the page below. Fill in the blanks on this page with the words called for. Then, using the words you have selected, fill in the blank spaces in the story. Now you've created your own hilarious MAD LIBS® game!

NOUN _____

ADJECTIVE _____

VERB _____

PART OF THE BODY _____

VERB _____

ARTICLE OF CLOTHING _____

OCCUPATION _____

A PLACE _____

NOUN _____

ADJECTIVE _____

PART OF THE BODY _____

VEHICLE _____

SILLY WORD _____

VERB ENDING IN "ING" _____

ADVERB _____

ADJECTIVE _____

Are you an aspiring drug kingpin who's looking to combine business

and _____ on your next trip to _____ South America?
          NOUN   ADJECTIVE

Then _____ no further. Bolivia is the premier travel destination
       VERB

for career-_____-ed criminals just like you! Whether you're
          PART OF THE BODY

a freelance _____-man traveling on a/an _____-string
              VERB   ARTICLE OF CLOTHING

budget or a/an _____ operating your own multinational
                 OCCUPATION

drug cartel, (the) _____ has something for everyone! Where
                    A PLACE

else can you visit a working cocaine _____, trade assassination
                                        NOUN

assignments with _____ dignitaries over dinner, and even see
                    ADJECTIVE

one of your former colleagues get hung by their _____ from
                                                 PART OF THE BODY

a/an _____? But don't forget work! No visit to Bolivia would
       VEHICLE

be complete without a visit to the _____-bamba region, where
                                    SILLY WORD

cocaine production is up and business is _____. So act
                                          VERB ENDING IN "ING"

_____! There's no _____ time to visit Bolivia!
   ADVERB   ADJECTIVE

MAD LIBS® is fun to play with friends, but you can also play it by yourself! To begin with, DO NOT look at the story on the page below. Fill in the blanks on this page with the words called for. Then, using the words you have selected, fill in the blank spaces in the story. Now you've created your own hilarious MAD LIBS® game!

ADJECTIVE _____

VERB ENDING IN "ING" _____

ARTICLE OF CLOTHING _____

PLURAL NOUN _____

ADJECTIVE _____

ANIMAL _____

PART OF THE BODY _____

NOUN _____

PART OF THE BODY _____

NOUN _____

A PLACE _____

NOUN _____

ADJECTIVE _____

SILLY WORD _____

PART OF THE BODY _____

PLURAL NOUN _____

ADVERB _____

TYPE OF FOOD _____

Adult MAD LIBS®
GINA MONTANA'S DIARY

The world's greatest ___gangster___ game

Dear Diary,

Today was a totally _____ day. I decided to go _____
                ADJECTIVE   VERB ENDING IN "ING"

at the Babylon Club because I just got this new _____
                                                  ARTICLE OF CLOTHING

with all these shiny _____ all over it. I look so _____
                         PLURAL NOUN   ADJECTIVE

in that dress, mostly because it's tighter than a/an _____'s
                                                  ANIMAL

_____ on me. Anyway, this cute _____ started
PART OF THE BODY   NOUN

grabbing my _____ on the _____ floor. So, we
               PART OF THE BODY   NOUN

headed off to the men's _____ to snort some _____
                          A PLACE   NOUN

up our noses. But then my _____ big brother, Tony, busted
                              ADJECTIVE

in on us! Well, I told him that I can _____ whoever I
                                         SILLY WORD

want! Then, he hit me across the _____ really hard. *Ugggh!*
                                   PART OF THE BODY

Big _____! _____, Manny was there to rescue
     PLURAL NOUN   ADVERB

me. And now I think I'm crushing on him because he's such a beef-

_____. Yum!
TYPE OF FOOD

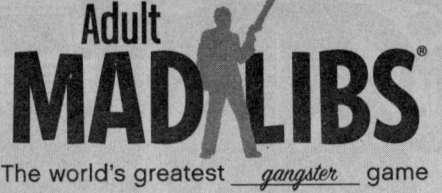

Adult MAD LIBS®

COCAINE: THE DOWNSIDE TO BEING UP

The world's greatest _gangster_ game

MAD LIBS® is fun to play with friends, but you can also play it by yourself! To begin with, DO NOT look at the story on the page below. Fill in the blanks on this page with the words called for. Then, using the words you have selected, fill in the blank spaces in the story. Now you've created your own hilarious MAD LIBS® game!

ADJECTIVE _____

PART OF THE BODY _____

VERB _____

PERSON IN ROOM (FEMALE) _____

FIRST NAME (MALE) _____

PART OF THE BODY _____

COLOR _____

ADJECTIVE _____

OCCUPATION _____

ADVERB _____

NOUN _____

VERB _____

PLURAL NOUN _____

VERB _____

NOUN _____

NOUN _____

PLURAL NOUN _____

Adult MAD LIBS® COCAINE: THE DOWNSIDE TO BEING UP

The world's greatest __gangster__ game

There's a good side and a/an _____ side to everything in life, even
                        ADJECTIVE

cocaine. Just ask Tony Montana. He's been snorting _____
                                                    PART OF THE BODY

candy for as long as anyone can _____. He'll tell you that coke
                                 VERB

can make you richer than _____ and more powerful than
                          PERSON IN ROOM (FEMALE)

_____ Castro! But Tony knows first-_____
FIRST NAME (MALE)   PART OF THE BODY

about how those pretty _____ lines have a/an _____
                        COLOR   ADJECTIVE

side, too. Sure, he's no medical _____, but he knows that
                                 OCCUPATION

too much coke can _____ affect your health. It can cause
                   ADVERB

_____ swings and the inability to _____, and it can turn
NOUN   VERB

your brain into _____. Plus, it can totally _____
                PLURAL NOUN   VERB

up your sex _____ and prevent you from having that baby
            NOUN

_____ you've always wanted. So listen to Tony! And don't do
NOUN

_____.
PLURAL NOUN

Adult MAD LIBS® SPANISH 101 FOR CRIMINALS

The world's greatest _gangster_ game

MAD LIBS® is fun to play with friends, but you can also play it by yourself! To begin with, DO NOT look at the story on the page below. Fill in the blanks on this page with the words called for. Then, using the words you have selected, fill in the blank spaces in the story. Now you've created your own hilarious MAD LIBS® game!

VERB _____

PLURAL NOUN _____

PART OF THE BODY _____

SILLY WORD _____

VERB _____

ANIMAL _____

NOUN _____

VERB ENDING IN "ING" _____

NOUN _____

PART OF THE BODY _____

Adult MAD LIBS® SPANISH 101 FOR CRIMINALS

The world's greatest _gangster_ game

Hola, clase! If you want to break into the 1980s drug scene in

Miami, you're going to need to _____ the lingo! Here are the
VERB

translations of some Spanish _____ that Tony Montana, AKA
PLURAL NOUN

Scarface, and his foul-_____-ed friends use a lot, so you can
PART OF THE BODY

be sure to blend in . . .

Cara Cicatriz: English translation: Scarface. Used in a sentence:

"Okay, Cara _____! You can _____, too. It makes no
SILLY WORD VERB

difference to me."

Chivato: English translation: An informant/stool _____. Used
ANIMAL

in a sentence: "Do you want a *chivato* on every street _____,
NOUN

watching everything you do?"

Yeyo: English translation: Cocaine. Used in a sentence: "Give me that

mother-_____ *yeyo* before I stick this loaded _____
VERB ENDING IN "ING" NOUN

in your _____ and kill you."
PART OF THE BODY

Adult MAD LIBS® — MANNY'S GUIDE TO GETTING WOMEN

The world's greatest _gangster_ game

MAD LIBS® is fun to play with friends, but you can also play it by yourself! To begin with, DO NOT look at the story on the page below. Fill in the blanks on this page with the words called for. Then, using the words you have selected, fill in the blank spaces in the story. Now you've created your own hilarious MAD LIBS® game!

ANIMAL _____

VERB (PAST TENSE) _____

ADJECTIVE _____

PERSON IN ROOM (MALE) _____

NOUN _____

VERB _____

TYPE OF LIQUID _____

NOUN _____

ADJECTIVE _____

COLOR _____

NOUN _____

PART OF THE BODY _____

NOUN _____

VERB ENDING IN "ING" _____

ANIMAL _____

PLURAL NOUN _____

VERB _____

Adult MAD LIBS®

MANNY'S GUIDE TO GETTING WOMEN

The world's greatest ___gangster___ game

Like Tony says, "Miami is like a great big _____ waiting to
ANIMAL

get _____." Tony may be _____ about some
VERB (PAST TENSE)   ADJECTIVE

things, but when it comes to women, _____ doesn't know
PERSON IN ROOM (MALE)

_____ from Shinola. After all, he even tried to get a girl by
NOUN

offering to _____ her ice _____. What a/an _____!
VERB   TYPE OF LIQUID   NOUN

He's not like me. I know all the _____ moves! I'm so into
ADJECTIVE

girls, I'm considering my own line of women's _____ jeans
COLOR

with my _____ written across the girl's _____.
NOUN   PART OF THE BODY

My signature _____ is _____ my tongue like a
NOUN   VERB ENDING IN "ING"

poisonous _____ that's about to strike! Of course, Tony's sister,
ANIMAL

Gina, is different. That's a girl you have to shower with _____
PLURAL NOUN

if you want to marry her. Just don't tell Tony we're in love or he'll

_____ me. *Shhhh!*
VERB

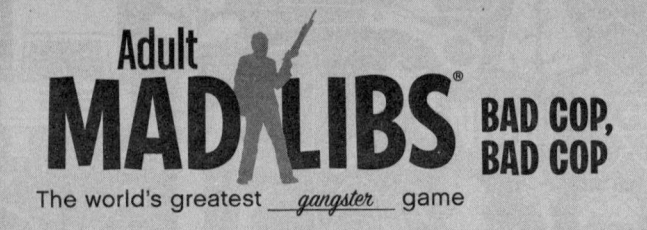

MAD LIBS® is fun to play with friends, but you can also play it by yourself! To begin with, DO NOT look at the story on the page below. Fill in the blanks on this page with the words called for. Then, using the words you have selected, fill in the blank spaces in the story. Now you've created your own hilarious MAD LIBS® game!

ADJECTIVE _____

ANIMAL (PLURAL) _____

COLOR _____

VERB _____

ADJECTIVE _____

ADVERB _____

OCCUPATION (PLURAL) _____

VERB _____

NUMBER _____

NUMBER _____

VERB _____

PART OF THE BODY _____

A PLACE _____

NUMBER _____

NOUN _____

PART OF THE BODY _____

ANIMAL (PLURAL) _____

Adult MAD LIBS®

BAD COP, BAD COP

The world's greatest _gangster_ game

Dealing with _____ cops like Mel Bernstein is just another part of
ADJECTIVE

the dirty business of dealing drugs! Paying off these _____ is the
ANIMAL (PLURAL)

only way to get the men in _____ to _____ the other
COLOR   VERB

way, so you can go about your routine of selling _____ narcotics
ADJECTIVE

and _____ killing competing _____ who are trying to
ADVERB   OCCUPATION (PLURAL)

_____ over your turf. Giving the cops _____ thousand dollars
VERB   NUMBER

every _____ days will prevent having to toss and _____
NUMBER   VERB

in your bed at night, worrying about whether tomorrow is the day

they will finally find you, put you in _____-cuffs, and throw
PART OF THE BODY

you in (the) _____ for the next _____ years! The only
A PLACE   NUMBER

other option is to become a/an _____-abiding citizen. And let's
NOUN

_____ it, that's not going to happen until the _____
PART OF THE BODY   ANIMAL (PLURAL)

come home!

WELCOME TO THE BABYLON CLUB!

The world's greatest _gangster_ game

MAD LIBS® is fun to play with friends, but you can also play it by yourself! To begin with, DO NOT look at the story on the page below. Fill in the blanks on this page with the words called for. Then, using the words you have selected, fill in the blank spaces in the story. Now you've created your own hilarious MAD LIBS® game!

ADJECTIVE _____

VERB _____

A PLACE _____

ANIMAL _____

NOUN _____

ADVERB _____

NUMBER _____

PLURAL NOUN _____

VERB _____

ADJECTIVE _____

VERB _____

NOUN _____

NOUN _____

NUMBER _____

Adult MAD LIBS®

The world's greatest _gangster_ game

WELCOME TO THE BABYLON CLUB!

Do you want to hobnob with the rich and _____? Then
_____ADJECTIVE_____

_____ on down to the _____ Club, the hottest   in
____VERB____   ____A PLACE____

Miami! Where the drinks are stronger than a/an _____, the
_____ANIMAL_____

cocaine is as pure as the driven _____, and the conversations
_____NOUN_____

are _____ tense! This is Miami's number _____ dance
____ADVERB____   ____NUMBER____

spot for all gritty, underage gangsters and the _____ who
_____PLURAL NOUN_____

_____ with them! We've got dancing clowns in _____
____VERB____   ____ADJECTIVE____

suits, comedians performing _____-out-loud jokes, and enough
_____VERB_____

_____-fire to satisfy even the most _____-happy gun
____NOUN____   ____NOUN____

enthusiast. And it's all here for you for just a/an _____-dollar
_____NUMBER_____

cover at the Babylon Club! Come for the food, stay for the assassination

attempts!

From ADULT MAD LIBS®: Scarface Mad Libs • Scarface is a trademark and copyright of Universal Studios.
Licensed by Universal Studios Licensing LLC. All Rights Reserved. Published in 2015 by Price Stern Sloan,
an imprint of Penguin Random House LLC, 345 Hudson Street, New York, NY 10014.

Adult MAD LIBS®

The world's greatest _gangster_ game

"HOW TO FAIL IN BUSINESS" BY FRANK LOPEZ

MAD LIBS® is fun to play with friends, but you can also play it by yourself! To begin with, DO NOT look at the story on the page below. Fill in the blanks on this page with the words called for. Then, using the words you have selected, fill in the blank spaces in the story. Now you've created your own hilarious MAD LIBS® game!

CELEBRITY (MALE) _____

ADJECTIVE _____

NOUN _____

PART OF THE BODY _____

PERSON IN ROOM _____

PLURAL NOUN _____

NOUN _____

TYPE OF LIQUID _____

ADJECTIVE _____

ADJECTIVE _____

PART OF THE BODY _____

NOUN _____

PART OF THE BODY _____

VERB _____

NOUN _____

Adult MAD LIBS®

"HOW TO FAIL IN BUSINESS" BY FRANK LOPEZ

The world's greatest _gangster_ game

I'm _____ and, for years, I led a/an _____ drug empire in
　　　　CELEBRITY (MALE)　　　　　　　　　　　　　ADJECTIVE

Miami. That is, until I met that no-good son of a/an _____ Tony
　　　　　　　　　　　　　　　　　　　　　　　　　　　NOUN

Montana! He stole my business and my girlfriend right out from under

my big _____! But maybe it's not all _____'s fault.
　　　　PART OF THE BODY　　　　　　　　　　　　PERSON IN ROOM

You see, after years of spending too much money on _____
　　　　　　　　　　　　　　　　　　　　　　　　　　　PLURAL NOUN

and popping the _____ off too many bottles of expensive
　　　　　　　　　　　　NOUN

_____, I got _____ and lazy. I started spending too
TYPE OF LIQUID　　　　　ADJECTIVE

much time watching my _____ league team and not enough
　　　　　　　　　　　　　ADJECTIVE

time being a cut-_____ businessman! So, if you want my advice,
　　　　　　　PART OF THE BODY

keep your eye on the _____, watch your _____, and
　　　　　　　　　　　　NOUN　　　　　　　　　PART OF THE BODY

_____ no one. If you don't, you might end up dead on your
VERB

office _____ like I did!
　　　　NOUN

From ADULT MAD LIBS®: Scarface Mad Libs • Scarface is a trademark and copyright of Universal Studios.
Licensed by Universal Studios Licensing LLC. All Rights Reserved. Published in 2015 by Price Stern Sloan,
an imprint of Penguin Random House LLC, 345 Hudson Street, New York, NY 10014.

Adult MAD LIBS

DIRTY LAUNDRY

The world's greatest _gangster_ game

MAD LIBS® is fun to play with friends, but you can also play it by yourself! To begin with, DO NOT look at the story on the page below. Fill in the blanks on this page with the words called for. Then, using the words you have selected, fill in the blank spaces in the story. Now you've created your own hilarious MAD LIBS® game!

PLURAL NOUN _____

NUMBER _____

VERB _____

SILLY WORD (PLURAL) _____

LETTER OF THE ALPHABET _____

PART OF THE BODY (PLURAL) _____

ADJECTIVE _____

NOUN _____

ADJECTIVE _____

PLURAL NOUN _____

VERB _____

ADVERB _____

ADJECTIVE _____

ADJECTIVE _____

NOUN _____

NUMBER _____

Adult MAD LIBS® DIRTY LAUNDRY

The world's greatest _gangster_ game

When you're rolling in so many _____ that you can't fit them
                                    PLURAL NOUN

into _____ duffel bags, you've got to find a way to make that cash
        NUMBER

_____ into thin air. Otherwise, those _____ down at the
   VERB   SILLY WORD (PLURAL)

FB-_____ might start sticking their _____
     LETTER OF THE ALPHABET   PART OF THE BODY (PLURAL)

into your business, so they can seize all that _____-earned
                                                  ADJECTIVE

money of yours. That's where _____ launderers come in. Sure,
                                NOUN

you can go to one of the _____ banks, and funnel funds into a
                            ADJECTIVE

myriad of fake _____, but that can get expensive. In this case,
                  PLURAL NOUN

finding a smaller operator to _____ your money _____
                                VERB   ADVERB

in a concrete basement might be the _____ way to go. That is,
                                       ADJECTIVE

unless that _____-time money launderer is also an undercover
               ADJECTIVE

_____. In which case, you're about to get a/an _____-way
   NOUN   NUMBER

ticket to prison!

Adult MAD LIBS® THE CUBAN CONSCIENCE CRISIS

The world's greatest _gangster_ game

MAD LIBS® is fun to play with friends, but you can also play it by yourself! To begin with, DO NOT look at the story on the page below. Fill in the blanks on this page with the words called for. Then, using the words you have selected, fill in the blank spaces in the story. Now you've created your own hilarious MAD LIBS® game!

ADJECTIVE _____

NOUN _____

PERSON IN ROOM (FEMALE) _____

VERB _____

NUMBER _____

NOUN _____

VERB _____

PLURAL NOUN _____

PART OF THE BODY _____

PLURAL NOUN _____

ADJECTIVE _____

NOUN _____

PART OF THE BODY _____

Adult
MAD LIBS® THE CUBAN CONSCIENCE CRISIS

The world's greatest _gangster_ game

Even Scarface has a/an _____ spot! And considering how
            ADJECTIVE

much he talks about having kids and starting a/an _____ with
                                                            NOUN

_____, it's no wonder he couldn't _____
PERSON IN ROOM (FEMALE)   VERB

up that family of _____ while on a business trip to New
                        NUMBER

York _____. Instead, he chose to _____ one of his
        NOUN   VERB

_____ in the _____ to spare the _____
PLURAL NOUN   PART OF THE BODY   PLURAL NOUN

of the family. And the _____ thing is, that decision ends
                            ADJECTIVE

up costing Tony his _____. Turns out, Scarface has a/an
                            NOUN

_____.
PART OF THE BODY

MAD LIBS® is fun to play with friends, but you can also play it by yourself! To begin with, DO NOT look at the story on the page below. Fill in the blanks on this page with the words called for. Then, using the words you have selected, fill in the blank spaces in the story. Now you've created your own hilarious MAD LIBS® game!

ADJECTIVE _____

CELEBRITY (FEMALE) _____

NOUN _____

PERSON IN ROOM (MALE) _____

SILLY WORD _____

ADJECTIVE _____

ANIMAL _____

NOUN _____

LETTER OF THE ALPHABET _____

NUMBER _____

NOUN _____

ADVERB _____

ADJECTIVE _____

ADJECTIVE _____

ADJECTIVE _____

NUMBER _____

NOUN _____

The spectacle of the climactic scene of *Scarface* is nothing short of

_____! First, the actress _____, who plays Tony's
ADJECTIVE   CELEBRITY (FEMALE)

little _____, tries to shoot _____ for killing
NOUN   PERSON IN ROOM (MALE)

her husband, Manny, while begging Tony to _____ her.
          SILLY WORD

Then, after each of Tony's _____ guards are killed outside,
          ADJECTIVE

he does enough cocaine to kill a/an _____ and makes a last
          ANIMAL

stand in his _____ using a/an _____-_____ rifle
    NOUN   LETTER OF THE ALPHABET   NUMBER

outfitted with a/an _____ launcher. It's at this moment when
          NOUN

he _____ storms out of his office and says the _____
  ADVERB   ADJECTIVE

Hollywood line, "Say hello to my _____ friend!" But, in the
          ADJECTIVE

end, even Tony's _____ weapon isn't enough to save him.
      ADJECTIVE

He ends up shot about _____ times and dies alone in a/an
          NUMBER

_____.
NOUN

Adult MAD LIBS® — THE WORLD REALLY IS YOURS

The world's greatest _gangster_ game

MAD LIBS® is fun to play with friends, but you can also play it by yourself! To begin with, DO NOT look at the story on the page below. Fill in the blanks on this page with the words called for. Then, using the words you have selected, fill in the blank spaces in the story. Now you've created your own hilarious MAD LIBS® game!

ADJECTIVE _____

NOUN _____

VERB_____

NOUN _____

NUMBER _____

VERB ENDING IN "ING" _____

NOUN _____

ADVERB _____

PLURAL NOUN _____

ADJECTIVE _____

NOUN _____

PART OF THE BODY _____

There's no doubt that *Scarface* has had a huge impact on _____

                                               ADJECTIVE

culture, the _____-film genre, and even on rap and hip-_____
            NOUN   VERB

music. In fact, since the _____'s release over _____
                               NOUN   NUMBER

years ago, the film has only increased in popularity among critics and

movie-_____ audiences. So much so that the movie is
           VERB ENDING IN "ING"

now considered a/an _____-mark of classic cinema. *Scarface*
                                  NOUN

has _____ stood the test of time! And whether you view the
            ADVERB

film as a means to glorify _____ or as a cautionary tale about
                                PLURAL NOUN

the dangers of _____ greed, one thing about the film can't be
                    ADJECTIVE

denied . . . the world will never forget . . . _____-_____!
                                            NOUN   PART OF THE BODY